For J. E. and Linda,

Hugs and happiness
always!

La Donna Meinden

4-14-02

W0006956

Angel
hugs

Angel hugs

Heavenly Embraces in Everyday Life

LaDonna Meinders

CHALICE
PRESS

ST. LOUIS, MISSOURI

Cover art: Chris Sharp
Cover and interior design: Elizabeth Wright
Art direction: Elizabeth Wright

This book is printed on acid-free, recycled paper.

Visit Chalice Press on the World Wide Web at
www.chalicepress.com

10 9 8 7 6 5 4 3 2 1   02 03 04 05 06 07

Library of Congress Cataloging–in–Publication Data

Meinders, LaDonna Kramer.
   Angel hugs : heavenly embraces in everyday life / by LaDonna Meinders
     p.   cm.
   ISBN 0-8272-0027-7
   1. Meditations. I. Title.
BV4832.3 .M45 2002
242 — dc21   2001005982

Printed in the United States of America

Contents

• •

Foreword

●●●●●●●●●●●●●●●●●●●●●●●●●●●●●●●●

What a delight to write a foreword for *Angel Hugs*! I have always believed words to be important symbols in our lives. In my life's work, words are the means of reaching people for God through my sermons and through my writing. Words are exciting tools. They can shape and sharpen, enlighten and inspire, while they generate energy and enthusiasm! I like Mrs. Meinders' subtitle, too: *Heavenly Embraces in Everyday Life*. As I have studied the Bible for many years, it has been my observation that time and again, Jesus embraced the ones whom society had rejected. Time and again, he restored their dignity. Today, more than two thousand years later, Jesus embraces all of us, rich and poor, educated or uneducated, well known or unknown.

There's nothing quite like a hug, is there? If we could begin each day with the idea that God sends us a very personal hug...an angel hug...wouldn't it be great? Wouldn't it make a wonderful difference in how that day goes? Mrs. Meinders has filled this little book with just the kinds of stories and words that will help make this happen for you!

You might like to know a little bit about the author. LaDonna Meinders is a woman whose beauty of spirit shines forth even beyond her outer beauty. In a life of sweet successes and her share of disheartening disappointments, from beauty pageants and glamorous concert halls to sweeping the sidewalk at a small newspaper, from a comfortable family life to that of single mother and job-hunter, Mrs. Meinders has developed an unshakable faith that she shares here in a dynamic, intimate way. Her gift is that of seeing God's love in everyday life, in the situations of ordinary people. These are the angel hugs with which she inspires, encourages, and uplifts the reader. A few minutes with this delightful book can help one face the day with renewed faith and confidence.

I have often said that creative words generate energy; negative words drain out energy. Try it and see. Your moments with *Angel Hugs* can be part of your daily spiritual vitamin pill!

Remember that enthusiasm, self-confidence, faith in God, love, all are contagious, and you can help spread them.

Remember, too, that God loves you, and so do I!

Dr. Robert H. Schuller
Senior Minister and Founder
Crystal Cathedral Ministries

Angel Hugs

• •

...and their children become a blessing.

PSALMS 37:26B, NRSV

His name was Maurice. He told me so, eyes dancing in his smiling face. He looked all of five years old.

After having lunch at the mall cafeteria, my parents and I were sitting at one of the park benches in the mall. Out of the corner of my eye I saw a couple of children playing, but the little boy's appearance at my side was a surprise.

"Hi," he said, and before I could answer, he hugged me! He didn't seem to notice my parents. I hugged him back, said "Hi," and asked him his name.

That moment stands out in my mind, and I am sure I will never forget it. To say that Maurice's hug "made my day" would be inadequate. I felt a warm glow of happiness from his impulsive act of love. This little boy had the gift of enthusiasm! The fact that he had never seen me before didn't stop him, nor the fact that his skin was black and mine white, nor the fact that decades separated our ages. After telling me his name, he flashed a huge smile and ran away.

Yes, sometimes the world crashes down around us. Sometimes people disappoint us and life is hard. These are often times when God sends us a hug...unexpectedly, and just when we need it most! It might be through kind, appreciative words spoken by a loved one, through the

• •

innocence and spontaneity of a little child, or through some brief, spectacular glimpse of beauty in nature.

I know Maurice was not an angel; he was not someone with supernatural powers. He was a regular boy, noisy and energetic like most boys. And yet his unexpected hug was like a little angel visit to me, reminding me of God's constant love and care.

I love little children, and it is not a slight thing
when they, who are fresh from God, love us.
CHARLES DICKENS

Thank you, God, for all the blessings, large and small, that you send me every day. Help me to be sensitive and to recognize these "angel hugs" when they come my way. Amen.

A Life of Thanksgiving

*Offer to God a sacrifice of thanksgiving, and pay
your vows to the Most High; and call upon me in
the day of trouble; I will deliver you, and you shall
glorify me.*

PSALMS 50:14–15

One thing many of us neglect is thankfulness. Oh, we
come running to God with our problems and heartaches,
and God helps us, but it's equally important for us to
practice being thankful! Thanksgiving isn't a one-day
holiday, but a way of life.

I recently began a ritual of listing three specific things
every morning for which I am thankful. I first got this
idea on October 9, which also happened to be the birthday
of my son, Joe, so my list that day began by thanking
God for Joe and all that he means to me. Besides listing
specific loved ones, my list often includes thanking God
for an answered prayer, some particular event that has
blessed me, or something in nature that seems especially
beautiful that day.

In this simple way, I have been amazed to realize how
much I have compared to how much I need. My goal is
to live a life of thanksgiving every day. I wish I could say
I never forget, but I do. When I remember to begin my
day this way, it's a lot harder to slump into a "poor me"
mood when something goes wrong later in the day.

A colleague of mine, when I was on the staff at
Oklahoma City University, used to read the morning

newspaper and then decide who she would most like to be that day and who she would least like to be! This is an interesting idea, and it might help us think about other people and step out of the rut of self-centeredness.

My admiration for the late Helen Keller began when I was eleven and read her book *The Story of My Life.* Here was a woman who could neither hear nor see, who learned to communicate and speak only through the tireless devotion of her teacher, Anne Sullivan. Helen Keller might have been forgiven for a spirit of bitterness. Yet, hers was a spirit of thankfulness, an indomitable and inspiring presence that thrilled and blessed millions— during her lifetime and afterward. Here was a woman who, in spite of profound handicaps, said, "So much has been given to me, I have no time to ponder that which has been denied." What a humbling and powerful lesson this is for me!

Thankfulness is a great leaven. It bubbles up and spills over. It brightens dark corners and erases small discomforts. It makes forgiveness easier and carrying grudges harder. Thankfulness always turns into an angel hug, because when we thank God, He warms us with His love. Thankfulness, like laughter, is better than medicine. Listing three things every morning is no sign of genius on my part. The only hard part is limiting it to three!

Gratitude is the sign of noble souls.

AESOP

Dear Father, my heart is full of thanks for all you have given me. For health, for loved ones, for happy memories, and most of all for your love, I humbly thank you. Amen.

4

A Thread of Hope

• •

*Hope does not disappoint us, because God's love has
been poured into our hearts through the Holy Spirit
which has been given to us.*

ROMANS 5:5

One of my most memorable experiences of a family trip
to Europe was seeing the tapestries that hung on the walls
of so many castles and museums. Even more than the
great paintings, the tapestries fascinated me.

At one house, we entered a room hung with large
tapestries, many of them several hundred years old. In
the same way that touching a piece of antique furniture
stirs the imagination, I found myself trying to imagine
the hands that held the threads when they were just that—
threads—before they became part of that work of art.

One day that tapestry existed only in the mind of the
artist who sketched it. Then a weaver studied the sketch
and worked with her threads until the picture became a
reality.

Looking more closely, I noticed something in the
tapestry: one thread running through the picture like gilt,
catching the light that poured in from the window behind
and lending a soft gleam to the whole scene. My mind
wandering, I began to imagine myself at a loom. The loom
was my life. In my hands were bobbins and threads of
every color, representing the individual moments of
my life.

• •

All of us are the weavers of our own lives. We have been given unique talents and precious moments of life, and if we use them faithfully, we can create something that will be a blessing to others, as those tapestries were to me. Like an artist, we must choose our colors with care. Dark despair and drab self-pity would not make a very pretty picture!

When we feel discouraged, we should try to remember that this moment is only a tiny part of the big picture, that the final result can still be beautiful in God's sight. Every act of kindness weaves beauty into life's tapestry. When you give someone your own angel hug through a word of encouragement or a smile, you are creating something beautiful. Someone you meet today may be hanging on to life by a mere thread. Your response in a caring and loving way may be just the slender thread that helps that person turn the corner from despair to hope.

Even if it is a little thing—do something for which there is no pay but the privilege of just doing it. Remember, you don't live in the world all on your own.

ALBERT SCHWEITZER

Lord, help me today as I continue to weave the tapestry of my life, that it may be meaningful and beautiful. Amen.

ce so completely that there was no room for such
. The man missed his old friend, but since there
 room he didn't invite him. Anyway, he stayed
 busy—what with feeding the grudge and
bering the place of its beginning. The only problem
at the grudge had no arms for shaking hands or
g checkers. Still, it was big and strong, and gave
n a certain security. It filled up the hollow spaces
ade the man feel bigger.

 time went by, the man continued to feed the
e, but he gradually began to forget about the place
beginning, and finally he could not remember it
hen he tried. The grudge was very heavy by now,
e man grew tired of carrying it around. In fact, he
 tired that his heart began to hurt again. Perhaps if
 thrown out the grudge, he could have lightened
d and reclaimed the place where hope, humor, and
eness used to live. However, this never occurred
, so he just grew older and more tired, carrying
udge everywhere he went. The story of the grudge
ly amazing; it is remarkable that anything could
from such an insignificant beginning to such great
d strength, which is all to the credit of the man's
 care and feeding.

get rid of an enemy, one must love him.

LEO TOLSTOY

*nly Father, please forgive me for any grudge I have
 in my heart. Where I have allowed feelings of
ment, help me to send out angel hugs, that I may
 the loving person you want me to be. Amen.*

Living the Beatitudes

*Seeing the crowds, he went up on the mountain, and
when he sat down his disciples came to him. And he
opened his mouth and taught them, saying: "Blessed
are the poor in spirit, for theirs is the kingdom of
heaven. Blessed are those who mourn, for they shall
be comforted. Blessed are the meek, for they shall
inherit the earth."*

MATTHEW 5:1–5

During the reign of Marilyn Van Derbur as Miss America,
I happened to be in a Minneapolis department store when
she made an appearance. I was eager to meet her because,
apart from the usual reasons, I had represented Oklahoma
in the Miss America pageant the year before. I waited
until her talk was over and was able to visit with her for
a few minutes.

In response to my question about how her year was
going, she told me a delightful story. It seems that she
was to make an appearance in a particular city, and her
chaperone booked a room for her in a fine hotel. Now, I
should tell you that Marilyn Van Derbur, even though
she had won a highly coveted title, was a down-to-earth,
friendly person whose beauty was more like that of the
girl next door. When Marilyn arrived at the hotel, the
maid was in her room.

"Honey, I've got to make this room extra nice, because
Miss America is going to stay here!" the maid exclaimed,
and went bustling about her duties unaware that that

very person stood beside her! I don't know how Marilyn introduced herself, but I am confident that her friendly, gracious manner was a memorable angel hug for the maid.

Do we sometimes look over the shoulder of the person we're with when someone a little more interesting comes into the room? Do we fail to recognize the value of true friendship just because it is familiar? Do we give more credit to glamour than to meekness? Marilyn Van Derbur made a lasting impression on me because she was so real. To me, she will always embody beauty, grace and, yes, meekness in a world where meekness is like a rare jewel.

True humility doesn't consist of thinking ill of yourself but of not thinking of yourself much differently from the way you'd be apt to think of anybody else.

FREDERICK BUECHNER

Thank you, Lord, for those people who really live the teachings of the gospel. Thank you for their example, encouraging me to become the person you would have me be. Amen.

The Grudge: A Fab

"So if you are offering your gif there remember that your broth against you, leave your gift the go; first be reconciled to your b and offer your gift."

A man and his friend, meeting disagreement. They called each o from one another, and parted in

The man was sad, and hu decided to go for a walk, and h place where the disagreement ha shadows lay a little grudge, the r The thing was poor and weak, ar noticed it, so insignificant did it a it surely would have died. The m and, holding it close to his hear where he lived.

The man gave the grudge a and particularly liked to rem beginning. The little grudge grev and sleek, and soon began to fill man lived. Before long, it crowde tender occupants like hope, hun

Frequently, the man saw his he felt a stirring to invite him in of checkers as in the old days, b

the pl things was n pretty remen was th playin the m and m

A grudg of its even and th was s he ha his loa forgiv to hin that g is real grow size a tende

To

Heave carrie resent becon

Purity

● ●

Finally, brethren, whatever is true, whatever is honorable, whatever is just, whatever is pure, whatever is lovely, whatever is gracious, if there is any excellence, if there is anything worthy of praise, think about these things.

PHILIPPIANS 4:8

We hear a great deal about pollution, the opposite of purity. Perhaps while we have been busy polluting our physical world, we have inadvertently polluted our society until that seems to be the norm.

Yet we sometimes sense purity in unexpected ways. A small flower, the falling of crystal white snowflakes, a phrase of music by Mozart, the innocence of a child's face...all bless us with simple, straightforward purity.

When my son Mark was in the eighth grade, we gave him a guitar for Christmas. After several months of lessons, he and a friend began to lead the youth group in singing the Psalms. Since the Psalms are written in poetic form, many of them make beautiful hymns. The voices of the young people singing these hymns were a bonus to our worship services. Besides, it was pretty neat to see them holding Bibles to read the lyrics! One of their favorites was from Psalms 19, which speaks of purity.

About the only time we hear that word today seems to be regarding the quality of things. We want pure air, pure food, pure water. We pay a premium for pure gold jewelry. But pure, as it relates to the human condition,

● ●

just doesn't seem to be "cool." Is it too simple for sophisticated tastes? Too goody-goody?

Purity has a way of cleansing. It scours away the hardness of our hearts and renews us. The King James version of Psalm 19, which Mark and his friend often sang, contains one of the sweetest descriptions of God's nature toward us: *the commandment of the Lord is pure, enlightening the eyes...sweeter also than honey and the honeycomb.*

Hearing these words, we feel a yearning deep within us to be connected with God, to feast on the honeycomb of His sweetness.

When our lives seem to fall apart or we feel overwhelmed by the pressures of a busy schedule, God embraces us every time we turn to His word. Reading those verses from Psalms is like being enveloped in a warm blanket. Thank God for this wonderful angel hug!

In prayer the stilled voice learns to hold its peace, to listen with the heart to silence that is joy, is adoration. The self is shattered, all words torn apart in this strange patterned time of contemplation that, in time, breaks time, breaks words, breaks me, and then, in silence, leaves me healed and mended.
MADELEINE L'ENGLE

Thank you, Lord, for your enduring love for me, for your peace and purity that bind up my shatteredness in a troubled world. Amen.

A Friend in High Places

●●●●●●●●●●●●●●●●●●●●●●●●●●●●●●●●●●

*There are friends who pretend to be friends, but there
is a friend who sticks closer than a brother.*

PROVERBS 18:24

You can get a good idea about the character of a person
by observing who her friends are. When we are young
our friends are a very powerful influence, and they help
mold us into the person we will become. Together with
those friends we make life decisions that set us on the
path we will follow. With friends we share secrets,
dreams, disappointments, and fears, multiplying our joys
and dividing our sorrows. With a true friend we can be
ourselves and know that we will be accepted. The quiet
moments shared with a friend give us comfort and
pleasure. Proverbs 17:17 tells us that "A friend loves at
all times." It is just that constancy that makes friends so
precious…the knowledge that someone will be there for
us in good times or bad.

Sometimes friendships get off-track. Feelings are hurt;
a careless remark causes misunderstanding. Sometimes
friends get busy and don't seem to have time for us. Or
we move to a new place and people are already so
involved with old friends that they don't include us or
even notice us. Loneliness really means friendlessness,
and loneliness has been aptly called the ultimate poverty.
Without that listening ear—that "friend who sticks closer
than a brother"—we feel isolated in a cold and hostile
world. Sometimes we feel that no one cares whether we

●●●●●●●●●●●●●●●●●●●●●●●●●●●●●●●●●●●●

live or die. Yet, there is always one who cares for us and wants to be our friend.

Joseph Scriven, who wrote the beautiful hymn "What a Friend We Have in Jesus," must have felt a great loss when his sweetheart drowned shortly before they were to be married. In utter loneliness, he turned to Christ and dedicated his life to helping needy people. When death took away his dearest friend, he turned to the One who will never desert us. In Christ he found solace, courage, and a new purpose for life, devoting himself to others who felt friendless.

If you are fortunate to have a true friend, today would be a great time to show appreciation to him. A personal note, an invitation to lunch at her favorite place, a small but unexpected gift, or just a friendly phone call, can help say "I care," "I love you," or simply "Thanks for being my friend." If you are estranged from someone who was once a dear friend, say a prayer first and then make your gesture of reconciliation.

Still, earthly friends may come and go. The Lord is our friend for all eternity, always ready to share our joys and carry our sorrows. His constant love comforts and sustains us. How wonderful to know that we can truly take everything to the Lord in prayer!

Friendship is not a reward for our discrimination and good taste in finding one another. It is the instrument by which God reveals to each of us the beauty of all the others.

C. S. Lewis

Thank you for my friends. Each one of them is truly an angel hug. I name some of them now and ask you to bless them today. And thank you, Lord, that I have a friend in Jesus, a friend who is able to transform all of my life's pain into beauty and strength. Amen.

Headin' Home

● ●

*"Let not your hearts be troubled; believe in God, believe
also in me. In my Father's house are many rooms; if it
were not so, would I have told you that I go to prepare
a place for you? And...I will come again and will
take you to myself, that where I am you may be also."*

JOHN 14:1–3

One of my favorite ski runs at Angel Fire, New Mexico,
where we occasionally took our children when they were
young, is a long, smooth run that seems to last forever. It
is called "Headin' Home." I like it because I can ski longer
without the hassle of lift lines and the interruption of
riding the lift. I can sail along and enjoy the quiet beauty
of the snow-covered mountains, relax on a not-too-
difficult run, listen to the swishing sound of my skis on
the snow, and, on the less crowded days, delight in the
near-solitude of that beautiful setting. On another level,
the name itself appeals to me. Headin' Home sounds
comfortable and right.

In the stillness of that experience, I have often thought
of a little girl named Callie. She was my aunt, and I have
heard many stories about Callie and her little brother,
Earl. Callie was sweet-spirited and good. One day, while
she was sitting in a chair in the "front room" with her
mother, she began to sing a little song whose words were
something like "Mama's got a home." At that time, the
family lived on a sharecropper farm in central Oklahoma
and their house was anything but luxurious. Times were

hard; the mother of the family often went to the cotton fields to chop cotton, or to drag the heavy cotton sack while she helped picked the crop.

When her mother asked Callie about the song, the child replied, "Oh, I don't mean this tacky place! I mean a home in Heaven with Jesus."

When Callie was four years old and Earl was two, Earl became ill with diphtheria. Shortly after this, in spite of the family's loving care and a visit by the country doctor, the little boy died. A few days later, Callie told the family she had heard Earl calling her. She died of the same disease soon afterward, but she left behind a legacy of sweetness, of absolute trust in God, and a simple faith in life after death that has survived her by more than eighty years.

Surely God does not want us to fear death, which is merely the doorway to a larger life with Him. Surely He wants us to look forward to a home that is better and happier than anything we have known on earth. Surely He wants us to sail along and enjoy the quiet beauty of that last run, to delight in the mountaintop experience of being ever closer to God, to trust Him when we are "headin' home" with a simple and child-like faith that strengthens us like an angel hug.

I never spoke with God,
Nor visited in heaven;
Yet certain am I of the spot
As if the chart were given.

EMILY DICKINSON

Thank you, Father, for sweet spirits like Callie who inspire us as we put our trust in you, now and forever. Amen.

Whiter than Snow

*Have mercy on me, O God, according to thy
steadfast love; according to thy abundant mercy blot
out my transgressions. Wash me thoroughly from
my iniquity, and cleanse me from my sin! For I
know my transgressions, and my sin is ever before
me. Purge me with hyssop, and I shall be clean; wash
me, and I shall be whiter than snow.*

PSALMS 51:1–3, 7

On a recent morning in church, as we prepared to receive
communion, I bowed my head to pray. I thought of the
things in my life that were not as they should be. As I
listed these things and prayed for forgiveness, a picture
suddenly popped into my mind. I had a vision of a giant
white cotton ball! All at once, I remembered the scripture
from the Psalms that speaks of being washed "whiter than
snow." It was one of those illuminating, "light bulb"
moments where something just clicks as a new idea pops
into the mind! In His wonderful, and sometimes
surprising, grace, God gave me a message of reassurance
and hope.

Based on my simple prayer of confession, God
forgave my shortcomings. Through my faith, Christ takes
me as I am: imperfect, spotted, and less than pure, and
makes me like a giant cotton ball! Though I grew up in
Oklahoma, which is one of the cotton producing states,
we didn't raise cotton on our farm, but I have learned a
little about it. Those puffy white balls don't grow that

way! When the cotton is picked it contains things that are not soft and white, such as bits of husk and stem that become brown and brittle. As the cotton is processed, extraneous material must be removed in order to make the cotton fine and pure.

I thought of this as I prepared to receive communion. God takes us in His great and gentle hands, removes the brittleness and impurities, and restores us to our finest form. All of this comes through His grace when we ask for forgiveness. I took communion, touching the silver tray along with the woman seated next to me as we shared, in that sacred moment, the wine and bread that represent our Lord's sacrifice.

We can't expect God to give us signs and visions every day. When one comes, it is an angel hug for which we can simply be thankful. I'm glad for the wonderful peace that comes from knowing that the Lord creates a new heart within us and makes us "white as snow."

Lord Jesus, I long to be perfectly whole; I want thee forever to live in my soul, break down every idol, cast out ev'ry foe. Now wash me and I shall be whiter than snow.

JAMES NICHOLSON

Thank you, Heavenly Father, for your forgiveness and peace, and for your great love that renews us. In Christ's name. Amen.

Love Letters

●●●●●●●●●●●●●●●●●●●●●●●●●●●●●●●●●●●

*In this the love of God was made manifest among us,
that God sent his only Son into the world, so that we
might live through him. In this is love, not that we
loved God but that he loved us and sent his Son to be
the expiation for our sins. Beloved, if God so loved
us, we also ought to love one another.*

1 JOHN 4:9–11

One day, when my son Mark was about fourteen years
old, I went into his room and happened upon a letter on
top of his desk. I have never been one to pry into my
children's personal things or read their mail. However,
this letter, lying there so openly, caught my eye and I
found myself unable to stop reading it, even though I
felt guilty…like an intruder into something special and
intimate.

What I found was one of the most beautiful love
letters I have ever read. Despite his youthfulness, Mark
had found a way to express the deepest feelings of his
heart, and to pour out those feelings in words. The letter
pledged his total love and commitment, as well as his
loyalty. This was not a one-sided thing; the letter was
full of appreciation for the love he knew was returned to
him. I felt a sense of wonder upon reading the words,
those words of a young and tender heart filled to
overflowing by the greatest power in the world: love.

The thing that made this experience so beautiful was
that the letter was written to God. With the directness of

●●●●●●●●●●●●●●●●●●●●●●●●●●●●●●●●●●●

a teenager, Mark told God how much he loved Him. I believe things like this are like a sweet fragrance to God. Sometimes we send hugs *to* heaven.

God writes many love letters to us. The fresh beauty of daybreak is a love letter from God; so is every rainbow, and tiny green buds on the trees every spring. God wants us to experience His love and goodness, but sometimes it's hard to get our attention. Maybe that's the way God felt 2,000 years ago when He sent us the greatest love letter of all time in the form of His son, Jesus Christ. When mankind continued to struggle and live in sin, God sent us a message we could understand. By the teachings and example of the Lord, we can begin to understand how much God loves us and how He wants us to live.

So faith, hope, love abide, these three;
but the greatest of these is love.

1 CORINTHIANS 13:13

Dear Father, I am humbled at the thought of your great love for me. I can think of no way to thank you except to offer my whole life as a love letter to you, honoring you with everything I say and do. Amen.

A Cherry or an Onion?

• •

*Butter and honey shall he eat, that he may know to
refuse the evil, and choose the good.*

ISAIAH 7:15, KJV

When my daughter, Lori, was three, she climbed up onto
a high snack-bar stool, discovered an interesting-looking
relish dish, and popped a bright red radish into her
mouth. Almost immediately, she spit it out, wrinkled up
her face in disappointment, and said, "I thought it was a
cherry, but it was an onion!"

Many years have passed, but this little scene has
crystallized in my memory. For one thing, it was a cute
saying. Parents tend to remember cute things their
children say and do. But more than that, it's a great
example of life's choices and their consequences.

Because she was only three, Lori was operating with
limited information. She knew cherries were small,
round, and red. Best of all, they were sweet. She also knew
that onions were *not* sweet, and were definitely
unappealing to her taste buds. What she got was neither
the thing she expected nor the thing she thought she had.

I remember understanding Lori's disappointment
and feeling motherly compassion that she got bitter when
she wanted sweet. Whatever else I might have felt, it was
one of those moments when we as parents sense the long
road of learning ahead for our children, the
disappointments that will come as the result of wrong
choices, the bittersweet journey toward adulthood.

• •

Don't you sometimes wonder how God must feel when He watches us reach for an expected sweet and grab the "onion" of wrong choices? How He must long for us to choose wisely and resist temptations, those alluring fruits that turn bitter on the tongue.

As parents, we experience joy (to say nothing of relief!) when our children grow up and learn to make good decisions. What a wonderful angel hug! In some shadow of the divine way in which God relates to us, I believe this joy in seeing our children do well is like His joy in us when we grow and learn to choose wisely. The best thing is this: God is our parent whose love is unconditional and never-ending. Whether with Lori and the radish, or the next decision you or I are called to make, He waits for us to choose the good, to taste the true sweetness of life He offers us.

Children have more need of models than of critics.
JOSEPH JOUBERT

Help me choose wisely today, Father, in all the decisions I make. Amen.

Confrontation

● ●

*He entered the temple and began to drive out those
who sold, saying to them, "It is written, 'My house
shall be a house of prayer'; but you have made it a
den of robbers."*

LUKE 19:45

I almost always try to avoid confrontation. But time after
time I've noticed that a bad situation only gets worse until
I face up to it. Once I take that step and talk it out with
the other person, resolution is often easier than I had
expected. Once again, the worry was worse than the
problem itself.

The women's movement has probably helped some
of us be more honest about our feelings and speak up for
ourselves. Still, at the risk of being called old-fashioned, I
believe most women lean toward the nurturing, accommo-
dating parts of their personalities rather than areas involving
conflict. At least, I am that way. Change isn't easy.

We want to be Christ-like, modeling our lives after
the Lord. After all, wasn't Jesus meek and mild? Didn't
the Old Testament prophets picture Him as a lamb before
its slaughterers? Didn't He go about "doing good,"
healing the sick, accepting the outcast, forgiving the
sinner, feeding the hungry, raising the dead? Yet we know
that this same Jesus drove the money changers out of the
Temple and stood up to the self-righteous Pharisees. Jesus
was no wimp! His kindness came from strength and
compassion, not from a fear of confrontation.

● ●

How far we have to stretch even to resemble Christ's example! For my part, I'm afraid I avoid confrontations because I fear the loss of that person's goodwill. Sometimes, maybe I'm just afraid the other person's logic will overwhelm me or that my argument will lead to ridicule.

Those of you who are parents know that we have to confront our children when we sense a real problem. Issues must be addressed, and at those moments personal popularity is not an issue; we must do what we know is right.

Confrontation isn't easy. God didn't promise that any of life would be easy. What He did promise is that He will always be with us, and that He will give us strength for every situation. By giving us the courage to confront, God sends us angel hugs that help us to be effective witnesses for Him.

To get out of a difficulty, one usually must go through it.

SAMUEL EASTON

Dear Lord, I pray for your peace, love, and joy. When I face confrontations, help me stand for what is right, and empower me by your Spirit. Through Christ I pray. Amen.

DAY

Using the Whole Mind

DAY
13

• •

*And one of them, a lawyer, asked him a question, to
test him. "Teacher, which is the great commandment
in the law?" And he said to him, "You shall love the
Lord your God with all your heart, and with all your
soul, and with all your mind."*

MATTHEW 22:35–37

An odd expression that I remember hearing as a child is
"half a mind." People would say they had "half a mind"
to do something or other. Sounds funny, doesn't it? I
suppose it reflected a thought that lolled around lazily
in the mind, not intentional or purposeful and, most
likely, one that would never result in action.

"Half a mind!" If we think about it, there's a message
in that phrase. It describes the way we sometimes go
about things in life…even important things.

When Christ was asked by the lawyer what was the
greatest commandment, He said, "You shall love the Lord
your God with all your heart, and with all your soul, and
with all your mind" (Matthew 22:37).

Why is it so difficult to love—or do anything else—
with the whole mind? Several years ago, I worked in the
Career Development and Placement office of a private
university. We worked with graduating students on their
résumés, helping them create the best possible impression
in order to get a job. It was amazing how vague some of
them were about their job objectives. For their job goal,

• •

they would fill in something like "To work in a medium-sized company."

Then we would have to say, "Focus, focus! Be specific. What is it you want to do in that medium-sized company?" Focusing keeps us from being splintered; it calls upon the whole mind to look in one direction. One can't focus with half a mind. The distraction of whatever else is going on in the other half prevents our thinking clearly.

In our Christian life, having "half a mind" to follow the Lord isn't enough. It's like trying to be halfway in love or halfway pregnant. At some point, each of us must commit our whole heart and soul and mind to the Lord in love. I know that my happiest times, when I especially felt that warm angel hug, have been times when I used my mind in a faithful, spiritual way: intentional, focused, and whole. Am I willing to fulfill Christ's commandment today and love Him with all my mind?

If a man is called to be a street sweeper, he should sweep streets even as Michelangelo painted, or Beethoven composed music, or Shakespeare wrote poetry. He should sweep streets so well that all the hosts of heaven and earth will pause to say, here lived a great street sweeper who did his job well.

MARTIN LUTHER KING, JR.

Help me, Lord, to think and act with my whole mind, that my life may be pleasing to you. Most of all, help me to love you with all my heart. Amen.

Without a Compass

• •

> *And the* LORD *will guide you continually, and*
> *satisfy your desire with good things, and make your*
> *bones strong; and you shall be like a watered garden,*
> *like a spring of water, whose waters fail not.*
>
> ISAIAH 58:11

Few things are as exhilarating to me as seeing wild geese in flight. I don't know why, exactly; perhaps it is the sheer beauty of their flight, the haunting sounds they make, or the sense of freedom I feel watching them. Whatever it is, seeing the geese in flight always thrills and inspires me.

My son John gave me a poster once that read, "Life is either a wonderful adventure or nothing at all." (This fantastic quote is from Helen Keller. What a woman! But that's another story.) The poster was significant to me because, at that time, I felt that my life wasn't much of an adventure. There was too little faith, too little living on the front edge of life, too little excitement and wonder. I believe this is true for most of us, much of the time. Maybe this is why seeing the wild geese is so powerfully uplifting.

Stretched across the open sky, the formation of the geese defies our understanding. How can they position themselves so perfectly without diagrams or directions? How could the leader of the flock, at the apex of their pattern, cross hundreds of miles through uncharted skies, dauntless in the face of weather or danger, always bearing straight toward his destination? This is, in a favorite word

• •

of our teenagers, awesome! With no power other than air currents, the tireless flapping of their frail wings, and an instinct given them by a loving Creator, the geese lap up the miles, following their leader through the change of seasons. Nothing could be more beautiful, and yet those frail wings, those slender bodies facing into the wind, demonstrate great strength and endurance.

I realize that Canada geese don't act on faith; they are simply responding to instinct. Still, there is something absolute and pure in their flight, their perfect formation an example of God's design of an orderly world. In addition to practicing trust, we Christians could learn from their example, in the way they take turns leading and the way their formation shifts the wind to let those in the rear rest a bit. How awesome is God's design! It inspires me to commit my way to God, grab hold of His hand, and soar!

One day you may see the geese flying overhead...a definite angel hug! And always remember, with God's grace, life *can* be a wonderful adventure!

> *All I have seen teaches me to trust the Creator for all I have not seen.*
>
> RALPH WALDO EMERSON

Thank you for the simple lessons of the wild geese, dear Lord. I know you will guide me, too, if I put my trust in you. Amen.

The Flight of Time

• •

I trust in thee, O LORD; I say, "Thou art my God."
My times are in thy hand.

PSALMS 31:14–15A

One morning I awakened from a deep sleep, possibly
from a dream, and saw that the clock showed 7:25. My
first reaction was to hurry to see whether John and Joe,
the youngest of my four children, were up and getting
ready for school. Then, a split second later and wide
awake, I realized that I needn't hurry. John is thirty-six,
married, and at work; Joe is thirty and also at work. These
things didn't happen yesterday, and yet in some recess
of mind while I slept, I had traveled back to another time.
For a few minutes I was nostalgic for the children who
grew up and went away. The empty nest is real, and
sometimes painful. But life today is good, as well. As
parents, we thrill to see our grown children building their
lives, confident in their adulthood. This is, after all, the
end result of our job during all those years of parenting.
If we were successful, a fulfilled and worthwhile
adulthood is where they will end up, not forever around
our table, although those memories are important and
we cherish them.

Time changes all of us as well as changing our
situations. Time has been described in many ways by
poets and philosophers, as sometimes a thief and
sometimes a benefactor. If we have no goal other than
pleasing ourselves and being loved, then time is a thief,

because it eventually separates all of us from those we love. But if our times are truly "in God's hands" our memories are like angel hugs that we can enjoy forever.

The remembrance of happy moments is one of God's best gifts to us, comforting and warming us. The remembrance of a loved one who is no longer with us brings hope when we believe that God will one day reunite us according to His promises.

Yes, I felt a momentary sadness when I awakened and realized that my children were no longer at home with me. Surely you've felt the same kind of nostalgia for someone. What can we do? We can say a prayer for that person, thanking God for every wonderful, special relationship we have enjoyed. Looking forward to these relationships in the future is also a joy!

Many people come and go in the course of a lifetime, as God blesses us with relationships that enrich us. Time is not an enemy or a thief, but a precious opportunity for us to experience God's grace, the changing moments merely down payments on an eternity of joy.

I don't know what the future holds, but I know who holds the future.

E. STANLEY JONES

Thank you, Lord, for memories of times gone by and for the hope you give me for the future. Help me to invest the precious moments of today in things of lasting value. Amen.

The Joy of Extravagance

● ●

"Give, and it will be given to you; good measure,
pressed down, shaken together, running over, will be
put into your lap. For the measure you give will be
the measure you get back."

LUKE 6:38

Extravagant! The word brings to mind other words: wasteful, spendthrift, prodigal…words we hope do not describe us, and certainly not words we associate with true joy. Most of us were taught—and teach our children—that extravagance is not good. "Turn off the TV when you finish watching it." "Don't throw away that gift-box. We can use it to wrap something else." "Don't put more on your plate than you can eat"— and the list goes on.

Our intentions are good. To waste anything on God's Earth is wrong. But what happens when this kind of frugality creeps into other parts of our lives? Parts where pure extravagance might be something wonderful? Parts where counting the cost (whether we are the giver or the receiver) is simply not appropriate?

We think of nature in her glory: a sunset in Boise, Idaho, bathing the nearby foothills with flaming beauty; the awe and power of a Kansas thunderstorm when brilliant streaks of lightning rip through a darkening sky; sunlight dancing on the waters of a clear, rippling stream in Colorado; your yard knee-deep in fresh snow, pure and crystalline on a winter morning; wheat fields turning

● ●

the plains into a sea of gold, rippling majestically in the Oklahoma wind; a forest of sugar maples in Vermont, afire with fantastic autumn colors. These things exult in extravagance, and uplift us by that extravagance.

Can you think of other ways extravagance might enrich your life and bless you? What about love? Love, more than anything, must be extravagant! The best love is boundless, giving totally, transcending measurements, forgetting the caution and limitations that constantly remind us of our own mortality.

Human nature seems to make us self-centered, asking, "What's in this for me?" Only when we look beyond ourselves can we give in a way that is truly free, and then we must have a heart big enough to withstand the inevitable disappointments that will come. But the reward is ours, too, the reward of making a gift with no hope for praise, like mailing someone a fabulous present...with no return address!

What we are really talking about is grace, the grace that enables us to give, and love, without expectations. When we do this, we become part of the love God showed us in Christ...extravagant love personified, the most meaningful angel hug we could imagine.

None are so poor that they have nothing to give...
And none are so rich that they have nothing to
receive.

POPE JOHN PAUL II

Father, I thank you with all my heart for the extravagant beauty of your world! Help me to be extravagant in good things according to your example. Amen.

• •

When Will We Get There?

● ●

This is the day which the LORD has made; let us
rejoice and be glad in it.

PSALMS 118:24

"Are we there yet?" "When are we going to get there?"

You who have traveled with children are familiar with these questions. It's natural for children to become restless.

We know that the trip could be fun for them if they would only appreciate the sights along the way. It's harder to recognize our own impatience, our tendency to "wish away" parts of life's journey.

Did you ever hear, "When I retire, I'm going to enjoy life…" "When the children are grown, we'll have more time for each other…" "When I don't have to work so hard, I'll become active in church…"

As we get older (and, hopefully, wiser!) we begin to understand that the ordinary things of life are really precious. The journey itself, not just a far-away destination, but the journey, is a fabulous gift from God.

Long ago, when farmers used horses to cultivate their fields and gardens, they often put blinders on them. These were stiff leather flaps that extended out beside each eye and prevented the animals from seeing each other, as horses usually worked in teams. The blinder kept the horse focused straight ahead with no distractions. That might have helped the horses, but how dull it would be for us! How sad if we were to put blinders on ourselves,

● ●

separating us from the noise, the lively distractions, the detours and discoveries, the surprises and delights of our life journey!

Heaven will come, but for now it is the ordinary moments that make up life, that make it so rich in memories and relationships. If today isn't special and wonderful, then when will life ever be special and wonderful? Every day, consecrated to God, can be a great day even if we haven't yet "arrived." Let's make an effort today to appreciate the ordinary things in life and thank God for them. Otherwise, *when are we ever going to get there*?

Nothing is worth more than today.

GOETHE

Thank you, Heavenly Father, for all the simple, ordinary moments today will bring. Help me to experience them with gratitude and to realize that angel hugs can come during the journey as well as at its destination. Amen.

Love: Gushy or Gutsy?

• •

> *Love is patient, love is kind. It does not envy, it does*
> *not boast, it is not proud. It is not rude, it is not self-*
> *seeking, it is not easily angered, it keeps no record of*
> *wrongs. Love does not delight in evil but rejoices*
> *with the truth. It always protects, always trusts,*
> *always hopes, always perseveres…And now these*
> *three remain: faith, hope, and love. But the greatest*
> *of these is love.*
>
> 1 CORINTHIANS 13:4–7, 13, NIV

Love. What a beautiful word! Many images come to mind when we think of this word: hearts and flowers, Valentine's Day, weddings, romance. There's the love for a spouse, child, or parent, and the love for one's country. Love can mean different things to different people.

Sometimes we use the word casually, as in "I just love lasagna," or going fishing, or whatever. We might use gushy or frivolous language to describe things we "love," when in reality, love is something of an entirely different nature. Deceitful flattery, the "gushy" expression of love, can turn our heads but lacks the stamina to sustain us through difficult times. A relationship built on superficial love will crumble at the slightest tremor.

In comparison, picture an elderly man sitting by the bedside of his wife of some fifty years, gently stroking her feverish forehead with callused hands. This is love that has weathered storms, trials, deprivations, happiness, and sorrow…and grown stronger for it. Maybe this man

• •

never found the words to express his profound feelings for his companion. Perhaps sentimental words felt awkward on his tongue. Yet his very life, his faithful presence, demonstrated these things to her.

My uncle died not long ago. He was 93 years young. Until his death, he always had a twinkle in his blue eyes, and a smile for everyone. He had a young wife: she was only 84! Uncle Ira was one of the few men I ever knew who truly liked to wear a necktie. Until he became ill, an impromptu visit to their house might find them in a friendly game of checkers, with him decked out in slacks, dress shirt, tie, and cardigan. Being with them and witnessing the love they shared was always an angel hug for me.

When Uncle Ira's health began to fail and my aunt could no longer take care of him, she took him to a nursing home, where she visited him at least once a day. He grew more frail daily and finally could not speak above a whisper. Then one day he looked at her and asked, "Fannie, when are we going to live together again?" So she took him home and cared for him, tolerating the interrupted nights' sleep, the lifting, and the constant care that would have exhausted a much younger person. He gained strength and flourished under that medicine known as love. When they said their final good-byes, that flame of love was strong enough to give both of them courage for whatever lay ahead.

Love is a powerful force, not a word to use lightly. We get a glimpse of the heart of God when we consider His love for us, the love that wants us to have life and have it more abundantly. Love! It is a word that

commands our respect, our commitment, our whole lives
in return.

> *Those who love deeply never grow old;*
> *they may die of old age, but they die young.*
> SIR ARTHUR WING PINERO

*Thank you, Lord, for those who demonstrate love by their
actions. Amen.*

Rest in the Lord

• •

*"Come to me, all who labor and are heavy laden, and
I will give you rest."*

MATTHEW 11:28

Rest. This is still another beautiful, comforting word! Rest,
in the most appealing sense, brings to mind the green
pastures and still waters of the 23rd Psalm. Many
passages of scripture speak of rest, of trusting God to
care for us when we are world-weary and out of sorts,
when we crave the healing comfort only our Heavenly
Father can give.

And yet, resting is not always easy. Resting requires
something of us; it requires letting go. The most expensive
mattress cannot guarantee a good night's rest if we are
stressful and tense. Only when we "sink in" and release
the tension of our muscles and minds can we achieve
full relaxation. Even God cannot give us rest unless we
let go, trust ourselves completely to His loving care, and
"sink into" His perfect rest.

One way of letting go is to visualize one's self in quiet,
restful surroundings. You might like to repeat in your
mind the words of the 23rd Psalm, taking the time to
imagine yourself actually lying down on the lush green
carpet of grass. Spend a few moments here, take some
deep breaths, and enjoy this before moving on. Now,
picture yourself being led ever so gently (by God's own
hand!) beside the still waters. Push all other thoughts out
of your mind and take time to enjoy the scene: the

sparkling clear water reflecting a blue sky dotted with fluffy clouds, the absolute quiet, the renewal one finds in such a peaceful setting. Again, take several deep breaths and thank God for this special blessing, trusting Him for the daily rest and care that you need.

Worry and stress often rob us of rest. What stressful things are keeping you from finding rest in God? Pause now, prayerfully, to think of these things, then with a deep breath and a sense of "letting go," release them one by one. With this action, entrust these cares to God. Try this deep breathing and letting go several times, until you actually feel a lightening and release of stress.

Do we believe God's word and trust His promise that He will care for us? By reading the simple yet wonderfully comforting words of the 23rd Psalm, we can experience the blessings of quietness, peace, and *rest*oration for the soul. Rest. What a blessed angel hug!

> *There is security and rest in the wisdom of the eternal Scriptures.*
>
> JAMES DOBSON

Dear Heavenly Father, thank you for giving us rest that restores our bodies and souls. Amen.

Simple Gifts

• •

> *When Jesus looked up and saw a great crowd coming*
> *toward him, he said to Phillip, "Where shall we buy*
> *bread for these people to eat?"… Another of his*
> *disciples, Andrew, Simon Peter's brother, spoke up,*
> *"Here is a boy with five small barley loaves and two*
> *small fish, but how far will they go among so*
> *many?" Jesus said, "Have the people sit down."*
> *There was plenty of grass in that place, and the men*
> *sat down, about five thousand of them. Jesus then*
> *took the loaves, gave thanks, and distributed to those*
> *who were seated as much as they wanted. He did the*
> *same with the fish. When they had all had enough to*
> *eat, he said to his disciples, "Gather the pieces that*
> *are left over. Let nothing be wasted." So they*
> *gathered them and filled twelve baskets with the*
> *pieces of the five barley loaves left over by those who*
> *had eaten.*
>
> JOHN 6:5–13, NIV

Do you think miracles could still be ours today if we were
to practice the same kind of trust as that little boy,
willingly sharing what we have to offer? The little boy's
lunch was a simple thing, but to him it was very
important. Perhaps his mother had lovingly packed it
for him. Knowing little boys, I can imagine that he never
completely forgot about it as the morning hours ticked
away, but savored the idea of how he would enjoy it when

• •

lunchtime came. Perhaps his stomach was beginning to grow a bit and his mouth just starting to water as the time drew near. I'll bet he could hardly wait to plop down on a nice, grassy knoll and enjoy his meal. Then something happened. The Teacher and His helpers began looking for food for all those hungry people and the little boy, in the innocence of youth, ran up and offered to share. Maybe you or I would have held back. *Is this loaf of bread really good enough to share with the Master? Are the fish too small, or not perfectly prepared? Is my offering so insignificant that I'll end up looking silly?* None of these thoughts bothered the little boy, who looked up at the Teacher with big, trusting eyes and offered what he had. It wasn't the value of the gift that contributed to the miracle but, rather, the complete willingness to share what he had.

Some person you meet today may need the miracle of your smile, the encouragement that only your voice can offer, the sharing of some particular insight that only you can give. Your personal angel hug will come when you respond willingly, just like the little boy in our story. Most of our gifts will not touch thousands of people, as his did. Some gifts will be known only by the person you help. Some gifts will be seen only by God—no Chamber of Commerce award, no *Time* magazine Man or Woman of the Year, no Pulitzer prize—just the simple joy of knowing you gave what you had, that you stood up for one helpless person, that you baked one needed casserole, that you were there when someone needed you. In my heart, I believe these are things of which miracles are made. These are the moments that give meaning and purpose to life, that turn the "little people" of the world into Heroes...Heroes of the Word.

We can do no great things, only small things with great love.

MOTHER TERESA OF CALCUTTA

Thank you, Father, for letting me help someone today. Let me give where I see a need, not seeking recognition but seeking only to share. Amen.

Don't Be Afraid of Failing

● ●

I can do all things in him who strengthens me.
PHILIPPIANS 4:13

Looking at the self-help books in the bookstore, and the titles displayed on the fronts of magazines, it's easy to see that we are a success-oriented society. Everyone seems to be offering new ways to find success, a sure cure to prevent failure. A book with a new angle to help us achieve success is likely to become a best-seller.

We want to do well for many reasons: financial reward, the "good life" for our families, personal satisfaction, or the respect of others. There is nothing wrong with working hard to reach our goals, but there may be something wrong with the way we look at failure, or perhaps our definition of it.

Could it be that we take ourselves too seriously? Sometimes we're so self-conscious that we refuse to try something new for fear of failing. This keeps us from many wonderful experiences. Tennis can be fun even if we only hit the ball every once in a while. Bridge can be interesting even before we learn all the rules of bidding. Could it be that the fear of "looking bad" is nothing more than conceit?

It is important to teach our young people that life tests us, that difficult times teach us more than the easy times, that our mistakes make more lasting impressions than the times when we "got it right" the first time.

● ●

The important thing to remember is that failing does not mean that we are failures, or that we will not reach our goal. All it means is that we didn't reach our goal *this time*. When we truly believe the promise in Philippians 4:13, *I can do all things in him who strengthens me*, we get a huge angel hug of encouragement that helps us keep going.

During the Winter Olympics, I always look forward to the women's figure skating competition on television. Several years ago Midori Ito, a young skater from Japan who was considered the best woman figure skater in the world, came to the Olympics as top contender for the gold medal. Her skill, particularly on the very difficult jumps, was outstanding. Throughout the week the press followed her closely and she seemed to feel very keenly the burden of representing her country…a country where "saving face" is extremely important. The stress began to show on her face and in her lack of concentration, resulting in several bad falls both in practice and in competition.

As the days passed, her chances for the top medal gradually seemed to slip away. She entered the final competition barely hanging on to a chance for a medal. On the final night, out there on the ice before thousands of spectators, millions of television viewers, and most importantly, the panel of judges, she took an ungraceful and embarrassing fall during what was to have been her most important jump. Now, Midori could have let her courage falter. She could have lost heart and given up, losing her chance for a medal. But that's not what she did. She got up, regained her speed, and attempted the most difficult and spectacular jump in her whole routine.

When she landed perfectly, the audience exploded in applause. Midori's face was beaming. She had faced her fear and overcome it. She did not let failure get the best of her. The result was a silver medal for this diminutive skater with giant courage, when the odds were that she wouldn't win anything at all.

One of my favorite quotes is from Dr. Robert H. Schuller, founding minister of the Crystal Cathedral: "I'd rather attempt something great...and fail, than attempt nothing...and succeed!"

Let's keep this in mind when we face challenges!

Far better it is to dare mighty things, to win glorious triumphs, even though checkered by failure, than to take rank with those poor spirits who neither enjoy much nor suffer much, because they live in the gray twilight that knows neither victory nor defeat.

THEODORE ROOSEVELT

Thank you, Lord, for accepting me and loving me even when I feel that I have failed. Help me to learn from my mistakes, and to keep on trying. Most of all help me remember that you created me and that makes me a winner. What an angel hug of encouragement! Amen.

God Gives Me Strength

•••

*Have no anxiety about anything, but in everything
by prayer and supplication with thanksgiving let
your requests be made known to God. And the peace
of God, which passes all understanding, will keep
your hearts and your minds in Christ Jesus.*

PHILIPPIANS 4:6–7

I am a pianist. Sometimes I perform as a soloist and
sometimes in concert with my duo-piano partner. Several
years ago, we were invited to play at a large convention.
We were performing Norman Dello Joio's exciting Suite
from the Ballet *"On Stage!"* which we had played many
times. We introduced the piece, sat down at the two
pianos, and the unthinkable happened! I played the
opening six notes and went blank. My partner awaited
her cue to begin. But I could not think of another single
note. I started over. The same six notes, then nothing.
Then a third time. The same thing happened. Finally, my
partner, who is also a dear friend and a person of great
positive attitude, said, "Let's play something else." We
did, and my memory was flawless.

Things like this happen occasionally to performers. I
have heard well-known concert artists get lost, or stop,
in the middle of a piece. This might be caused by fatigue,
by some distraction that causes them to lose their
concentration, or simply that vague thing known as
mental block.

•••

The best teacher I ever had once told me that I must take some spiritual time before every performance. She was right. I would not think of playing without taking time to ask God to give me clarity of mind, concentration, and inspiration.

One passage of scripture, the verses from Philippians printed above, has become my "formula" for peace of mind. Perhaps it would be helpful to you when you face times of stress, whether yours might be making a speech, teaching a class, chairing a meeting, or anything else. Let's look at it together:

Have no anxiety about anything. That pretty well covers it, doesn't it? Whether we have stage fright about making a speech, talking to the boss for a raise, teaching a class, or playing a concert, here's where we start. Pray specifically that God will take away your anxiety.

In everything by prayer and supplication with thanksgiving let your requests be made known to God. In everything. There's no problem too small for us to take to God, just as there's nothing too great for Him. Make your request, but do it humbly (supplication) and don't forget to thank Him for what He has already done.

And the peace of God, which passes all understanding, will keep your hearts and your minds in Christ Jesus. This part is the most sublime reassurance that God will truly help us. Think of the first part: God's peace is more than we can know or even understand. It is greater than our need. In Christ Jesus, we can rest assured that He will uphold us.

"Keeping our heart" says to me that my emotions and fears will be quieted by His unfailing peace. The next part, *"keeping our minds"* means to me that even in a place where my own mind might fail, where I might play six

notes and forget, God, who created me and who is greater than my mind, will sustain me.

I am thankful for music, and thankful when God allows me to be a blessing to others through music. Most of all, I am thankful for the strength I find in Christ to do this through the promise of His word. You have your own special gifts, your own ways of inspiring and enriching others. God will give you the courage you need to do your best. He will keep your heart and mind in Christ Jesus.

The Lord will give strength to His people;
The Lord will bless His people with peace.
Psalms 29:11, NKJV

How can we ever thank you for answering our prayers? We know we can trust you with the anxieties and fears of our lives, and that you have promised to give us peace. For all the answered prayers, all the promises you keep, all the angel hugs you send us, we thank you, Lord! Amen.

On Tiptoe at God's Window

● ●

A parable of grace and redemption

> *How precious is thy steadfast love, O God! The*
> *children of men take refuge in the shadow of thy*
> *wings. They feast on the abundance of thy house,*
> *and thou givest them drink from the river of thy*
> *delights.*
>
> PSALMS 36:7–8

The family is seated around the dinner table. Soft lights
cast a gleam on exquisite silver and crystal. Platters
heaped with the most beautifully prepared foods give
off a wonderful aroma. At the head of the table, the father
takes each plate and fills it generously before passing
it on. The room is filled with the excited, happy
conversation of people who know each other well. In the
background, music plays softly.

Two young beggars, a boy and a girl, stand at the
window, dirty faces pressed against the glass, their eyes
fairly bulging with amazement at what they see, their
stomachs growling with the presence of their constant
companion, hunger. They cannot even imagine
themselves seated at such a table, enjoying such a feast,
being served lovingly by a father who obviously cares
for them.

The little girl, Grace, nudges her brother. "Let's knock
on the door," she says.

"No. Are you crazy? They'd just throw us out!"

"But they look so nice!"

● ●

"Sure, they look nice. But we wouldn't fit in."

"But maybe if we apologized for how we look, for the dirty clothes and all, we could fit in." Grace's eyes grow dreamy. "See that girl, the one in the white dress? I'd like to look like that. Oh, just once, I would love to wear a dress like that!"

"Grace, don't be silly. Even if you put on new clothes, you'd still be dirty."

Grace was thoughtful. She was younger, and still hopeful. But her brother would not relent, and so she finally sank down beneath the window and fell asleep, her tears having washed a single clean track down each small cheek.

As she slept, she began to dream. She dreamed that the father looked toward the window and saw her. She dreamed that he ran to the door, threw it open, and invited her in. She dreamed that she had a hot bath with sweet-smelling soap. Then she put on a beautiful white dress and looked into the mirror. She looked like a new person, sparkling clean from head to toe! Overjoyed, she ran down the steps, to discover that the family had set a place for her. A place at their very own table! Joyfully she took her place with the family and began to share in the meal. With each bite, she felt strengthened and renewed. Best of all, she felt accepted and loved. Then she realized that it was not just a dream; it was real! Suddenly, she remembered her brother. He was still outside, looking in with bitterness and longing. Over and over again, she ran to the door to call out to him that he was welcome, but he didn't believe her and just turned his back in despair. Finally, the father sent his son to the door, thinking the boy might listen to him. The boy felt awkward and dirty, but the son assured him that his father would welcome him, that he, too, could be washed and renewed. At last the boy accepted the invitation. It felt wonderful to be included in the family! Overflowing with joy, the boy wondered why he had waited so long to accept the father's love.

The father smiled at him. "It's all right, my son," he said. "You are my child now, and you will always have a place at this table."

> *God hears the faintest cry of the sick, the lonely, the despised of the world. And he cares—deeply—about each one.*
>
> JAMES DOBSON

Dear Father, thank you for making a place for me at your table. Thank you that your love for me is greater than any dream I could ever have. Help me share that love with those who are still looking through the windows of fear and disbelief, who have not accepted your cleansing forgiveness and salvation, that they may come to realize the wonderful blessings...the unending angel hugs...of being part of your family. Amen.

The Pearl of Great Price

• •

> *"Again, the kingdom of heaven is like a merchant in
> search of fine pearls, who, on finding one pearl of
> great value, went and sold all that he had and
> bought it."*
>
> MATTHEW 13:45–46

I know a man who is fabulously successful, who built a
great and powerful business without financial backing,
literally starting up in his garage. He is the epitome of
the American dream and entrepreneurial spirit.

This man put everything he had into his venture. All
of his time, energy, talent, and imagination went into
building his business. He believed in it even when
everyone else told him it would fail. He believed in it
enough to give everything for its growth. It wasn't easy,
but it was the "pearl of great price" for which he gave all
that he had.

I find this story inspiring because he has something I
seem to lack. I dream great dreams and make impressive
plans but often find that I lack the fortitude to see them
through. I think many of us are like that. A famous
violinist had played a spellbinding concert. Afterward, a
woman, one of the many fans who came backstage to
greet him, said, "Oh, I would give half of my life to be
able to play like that!" The violinist surprised her by
saying, "Madam, that's just what I've done!"

Success doesn't happen by accident. We don't just
"fall into" good fortune. Ask a successful person about

his luck, and he will probably tell you that he made his own luck.

When we believe in something, we have to take a stand and pay the price. When we find our "pearl of great price," we must seize the opportunity and act on it.

There are many inspiring stories of men and women who have stayed true to their dreams. These stories enrich and uplift us like an angel hug. Joyce Hall, the founder of Hallmark Cards, was a high school dropout. At age 18, he boarded the train for Kansas City and started calling on drugstores, bookstores,and gift shops. All he had was a dream and two shoeboxes crammed full of postcards. He stayed true to his dream and became a success, with his company eventually selling in excess of $2 billion annually. I wonder what would happen if we applied this same tenacity to our faith!

Imagine the joy of the man in the parable when he was finally able to make the pearl his own! Do you think for one minute that he ever regretted his decision? Or do you believe, as I do, that he rejoiced in his treasure and forgot about what he had given up? An important part of this story, which we might easily overlook, is that the man *knew what he was about*. His business was pearls, but he didn't just stumble onto them. He went *in search of* fine pearls, and he did his homework; he knew a good pearl when he saw one.

> *Every man also to whom God has given wealth and possessions and power to enjoy them, and to accept his lot and find enjoyment in his toil— this is the gift of God.*
>
> ECCLESIASTES 5:19

Dear Lord, you know me even better than I know myself. You know that I often lack courage and try to take the easy way. Help me be willing to pay the price for things of true worth and to recognize those things when they come along. In Jesus' name. Amen.

Mountaintop Memories

● ●

*When the LORD saw that he turned aside to see, God
called to him out of the bush, "Moses, Moses!" And
he said, "Here am I." Then he said, "Do not come
near; put off your shoes from your feet, for the place
on which you are standing is holy ground."*

EXODUS 3:4–5

Holy ground still exists today. In fact, where you are right
now is holy ground! It's where you start, no matter where
you're going. It could be your own personal burning bush
from which God speaks to you. This was surely one of
the "mountaintop" experiences in Moses' eventful life!

We all have mountaintop experiences. Yours might
have been around the campfire at church camp long ago,
or the moment when you accepted Christ, or some other
moment when you felt God's presence in a special way.
I've had those moments, those times so thrilling and
inspiring that I felt I should take off my shoes even as
Moses did. We can all be thankful for those times. They
nourish us in an unseen way, strengthening us for the
times of testing when our faith might falter.

Sometimes these special moments catch us unawares.
I was in the labor room with my son and daughter-in-
law before the birth of their first child. Like many couples,
they had attended childbirth classes where my son
learned to be his wife's coach for the breathing techniques
that would be used during labor. In that small room I felt
a sense of awe— even of reverence— as we awaited one

● ●

of God's greatest miracles, the birth of a child. Even more, I was keenly aware that I was witnessing an intimate and special thing as I watched these two interact...hearing the encouragement in his voice that immediately calmed her, recognizing the love and trust they had built in six years of marriage. This love and trust, and their faith in God, will carry them through the tough times of parenting in a world that has become increasingly difficult for the family unit.

We can't make mountaintop experiences happen. We probably will stumble upon them unpredictably as we travel through the hills and valleys of life. Maybe you are in a valley right now. Maybe you find it difficult to lift each foot to take the next weary step. Maybe you have lost the enthusiasm you felt as a new Christian. But keep on going! Keep the faith, and stay tuned to God. A mountaintop experience may be just over the next hill. Then God will bless you with an angel hug, a new viewpoint, and new inspiration. He will restore your soul and give you strength. He will fill you with awe for the beauty and wonder of His great creation. And when He does, remember that you are standing on holy ground.

Let never day nor night unhallowed pass, but still remember what the Lord hath done.

WILLIAM SHAKESPEARE

Heavenly father, I give myself to you in this moment, in this particular place where I am. Thank you for special moments when I feel your presence so close to me, and help me realize that even I can stand on holy ground. Amen.

Consider the Lilies

• •

> *"And why are you anxious about clothing? Consider
> the lilies of the field, how they grow; they neither toil
> nor spin; yet I tell you, even Solomon in all his glory
> was not arrayed like one of these."*
>
> MATTHEW 6:28–29

Have you ever been so distraught that you sat down with
your Bible in hand, hoping to open it at random to a
passage that would somehow help you? I have, and while
I would be the first to say this doesn't take the place of
serious Bible study, I'd like to tell you a true story.

A number of years ago, I found myself needing a new
winter coat. At that time we had four children at home
and a coat was an important purchase, not one to be taken
lightly. This was after the mini-skirt craze, and women's
hemlines had done a dizzying swing that included the
extra-long styles and everything in between. I couldn't
decide what kind of coat to buy, and as the days passed
the question became almost an obsession. In the
department store, I would look at rack after rack of coats
and become even more confused. What length coat did I
want? Did I want a bright color or a neutral? Did I want
a fake fur or a plain coat? The more I worried, the more
this question took over my conscious thoughts. Finally,
disgusted with myself for being consumed by such a
trivial matter, I decided to pray about it. I picked up my
Bible, and prayed as I opened it at random. The words of
Isaiah 3:18–26 jumped out at me like a bolt of lightning!

• •

I didn't know there was such a chapter in the Bible; it listed everything women wore in those days, from cloaks and robes right down to jewelry and perfume! I was stunned, but even more, I felt an overwhelming sense of the presence of God as He answered my prayer. Suddenly, a new coat didn't seem so important as I was reminded—in a way that left no room for doubt—that outward finery doesn't mean anything in the big scheme of things.

Sometimes we might feel that we shouldn't "bother" God with our prayers about little things. Praying about what kind of coat to buy doesn't seem very important. But God didn't say, "Why is LaDonna praying about a coat when she must realize there are wars going on and people starving?" No. He met me at my need. God will always meet you at your need, in every area of life. No question is too big or too small to bring to Him.

You may wonder about the coat; well, to finish the story, I will tell you that I found one. The next time I was in the department store, it practically "jumped out" at me. It was a long coat, warm and elegant, and I wore it for years. It was perfect. But the important thing is that when I found it, I was no longer obsessed with it. My mind was freed to think about other things.

I will never forget that encounter with God, when I discovered an amazing scripture He revealed to me in such a personal way. I felt thankful and humble that He helped me rise above my problem. The angel hug is that He is always there, to help with every problem we have.

Let it be the hidden person of the heart with the imperishable jewel of a gentle and quiet spirit, which in God's sight is very precious.

1 PETER 3:4

Dear Heavenly Father, you know my needs, and right now I turn them over to you. Help me learn to distinguish between the important and the unimportant as I seek Christ's Kingdom and His righteousness. Amen.

Humility

• •

*"But when you are invited, take the lowest place, so
that when your host comes, he will say to you,
'Friend, move up to a better place.' Then you will be
honored in the presence of all your fellow guests. For
everyone who exalts himself will be humbled, and he
who humbles himself will be exalted."*

LUKE 14:10–11, NIV

After twenty-three years of marriage, I found myself
facing a divorce. I had been a stay-at-home mom, which
I suddenly came to recognize as a genuine luxury. Other
than teaching piano in my home studio, I had never had
a job and now, at just over 40, I faced the terrifying
prospect of job-hunting. My talents, besides music, lay
in the field of writing and words, so I applied at the local
newspaper and was delighted to get a job proofreading
and selling ads. It was not easy. I was a good reader but
didn't realize that proofreading was different; when we
read, we skim over words and our minds fill in the blanks.
Proofreaders have to look at every word and cannot allow
the subconscious mind to fill in blanks, as I learned the
hard way when the editor called me in after the first week
and showed me some glaring mistakes in a front-page
headline. And selling ads to the local businesspeople in
our small town, most of whom I had known for years in
social situations, took courage. It was hard not to feel
personally rejected if a friend didn't take out a big ad!
Then there was the matter of working with, and for,

people who were much younger than I. If I expected them to defer to me I was wrong. But the most difficult thing for me, and probably the thing that taught me the most valuable lesson, was when it came my turn to sweep the sidewalk in front of the newspaper office.

Each of us has a certain image of ourselves, and sometimes it's not very accurate. Mine was shaped by many things: I had been Miss Oklahoma; I had a college degree; my husband had been in politics, and we had socialized with governors and senators. Not only that, but I think our family had an exaggerated idea of our importance in our small town. My face burned with humiliation as I took the broom and headed out the front door of the newspaper office. I did the job as quickly as I could, hoping none of my friends would see me. I felt the same when it was my turn to fill the newspaper dispenser at the supermarket, where the entire town seemed to be going in and out.

I survived the job and the divorce, and I learned a lot. As I gradually overcame my sensitivity, I began to see things in perspective. I learned that being older doesn't necessarily mean being smarter. I learned that punching a time clock was OK, and that it felt good to pick up my check and pay bills. I developed a sense of humor and was able to laugh at myself for not knowing that "FYI" on a memo meant "for your information" and, when I needed a paper punch, looking for a little hand-held gadget like the one in my "junk drawer" at home and not recognizing the long, sleek device that punched three holes at once. As I moved on to better-paying jobs I realized that they had more prestige, but my actual work was no more honorable than when I had been asked to sweep the sidewalk. Every job is important! When we are too full of ourselves, it's hard to think of ourselves as team players.

I think I am wiser and more compassionate because of these important experiences. I will always be grateful to the newspaper publisher who hired me, green as grass, for that first job.

God has a plan for your life and mine, and we can fulfill that plan if we don't let pride hold us back. But don't pray for humility unless you are ready to use that broom…or whatever task He has in mind for you. When we can finally learn to be thankful for humble tasks, we are ready for the big angel hug that will surely come our way!

> *O grant me, Heaven, a middle state,*
> *Neither too humble nor too great;*
> *More than enough, for nature's ends,*
> *With something left to treat my friends.*
>
> DAVID MALLET

Dear Lord, I confess my pride. Perhaps it's because I feel inadequate or afraid that I tend to act important. Help me to walk in humility even as Christ was humble and made Himself a servant to others. In His name I pray. Amen.

Teenagers Don't Keep

• •

> Unless the LORD builds the house, those who
> build it labor in vain...Lo, sons are a heritage
> from the LORD, the fruit of the womb a reward.
> Like arrows in the hand of a warrior are the
> sons of one's youth.
>
> PSALMS 127:1A, 3–4

Coming home from work, I noticed a small white card
on the porch as I unlocked the door. Picking it up, I saw
a muddy smudge on one corner and decided it had blown
over from someone else's yard. It was a business card,
with the name of a caseworker for the Department of
Human Services, better known as the Welfare
Department. Certain that the card was meant for someone
else, I laid it aside. However, a phone call several days
later confirmed my barely acknowledged fears that the
card was, indeed, meant for me. Yes, some concerned
neighbor had called DHS, worried that Joe was alone too
much and getting into trouble. Could this happen to my
curly-haired, adorable Joe, the youngest of my four
children whom I love more than life itself? How did our
perfect family get to this point?

Joe's world fell apart when his father and I divorced.
Not only was Dad gone, but his three older siblings had
grown up and gone, too, including his best buddy/big
brother John, who had just entered college. Add to that
the turbulence of puberty. Then I dragged him, kicking
and screaming, away from the emotional security of our

• •

small town to a big city and new school where he didn't know even one person. See Dad go away. See Mom go to work. See Mom date. See Mom go to night school. See Joe home alone. All of this was at a time when an adolescent boy needs the most reassurance and affirmation.

Yes, Joe was in trouble. I dropped him off at school every morning and saw him enter the front door. I didn't see him walk through the halls, out the back door, and home again. Here he spent most days watching TV, working on his motorcycle, or baking brownies.

When his teachers told me he was cutting classes and failing, I (being the modern and dutiful mother) whisked him off to a counselor. The verdict? Joe was lonely.

It's so easy to rationalize in order to make things appear the way we want them to. Surely my dating didn't hurt Joe. After all, we often included him…My job at the University offered tuition remission for graduate school. Who wouldn't jump at the chance for an MBA? My son missed his friends so much, why not let him spend weekends in our old hometown with his friends? After all, his grandparents could keep an eye on him…

Teenagers don't keep. If they aren't carefully tended, they get into trouble. I think the thing that (barely) saved us was our quiet time every night when I sat on the side of his bed to hear his prayers and tell him I loved him. But I was not the mother I should have been. Joe needed more from me than he got, and while this story is painful to tell, I hope it will help others get their priorities straight. Today Joe is a young man, a sensitive and good person. Someday, I pray, he will find the right young lady and have a family of his own. I believe, given his unique history, he will be a good and loving father. I also pray that he will remember with forgiveness the long and lonely days when I was "too busy."

Is there someone in your life who is silently crying out for your attention? If so, are you willing to put other things on the back burner so you can be available? Children truly are a heritage from the Lord, and that heritage deserves our best efforts. When we give our children our best attention, the angel hugs we get are not temporary; they are eternal.

Children begin by loving their parents;
As they grow older they judge them;
Sometimes they forgive them.

Oscar Wilde

Father, please guide me today as I prioritize my time. Help me to be faithful to the duties you have given me. For the times I was not faithful in the past, I ask your forgiveness. In Jesus' name. Amen.

Wise or Foolish?

•••

> *"At that time the kingdom of heaven will be like ten
> virgins who took their lamps and went out to meet
> the bridegroom…At midnight the cry rang out:
> 'Here's the bridegroom! Come out to meet him!'
> Then all the virgins woke up and trimmed their
> lamps. The foolish ones said to the wise, 'Give us
> some of your oil; our lamps are going out.' 'No,' they
> replied, 'there may not be enough for both us and
> you. Instead, go to those who sell oil and buy some
> for yourselves.' But while they were on the way to
> buy the oil, the bridegroom arrived. The virgins who
> were ready went in with him to the wedding
> banquet. And the door was shut. Later, the others
> also came. 'Sir! Sir!' they said. 'Open the door for
> us!' But he replied, 'I tell you the truth, I don't know
> you.' Therefore keep watch, because you do not know
> the day or the hour."*
>
> MATTHEW 25:1, 6–13, NIV

Earlier this week, I drove some sixty miles to Stillwater,
Oklahoma, to have lunch with my son Mark. It was a
beautiful March day. My car purred along, and I enjoyed
the lovely, rolling countryside of central Oklahoma. Trees
were beginning to bud, promising an early spring. I felt
happy and carefree as I lapped up the miles, listening to
my favorite classical radio station.

•••

Two hours later, after telling Mark good-bye, I mentioned that I needed to buy gas. He directed me to a convenience store on my way out of town.

I had good intentions, but there was an obstacle: A detour sign stood between that particular store and me, so I headed out of town. The Interstate was only ten miles down the road, and I remembered a station somewhere along that road. Actually, I passed several other stations, but I didn't stop. They were on the other side of the highway and didn't seem convenient.

As I cruised along toward the Interstate, my gas gauge showed six miles. The classical music played, and the budding trees waved their branches.

Five miles later, with no station in sight, I turned off the air conditioner to conserve fuel. Now my digital readout showed one mile to go. I turned off the radio to concentrate on my predicament. I started to pray...and to sweat. I pictured myself stranded along the highway. Yes, I would feel foolish, but even worse was that I might be in peril. Should I sit in my car and wait for a highway patrolman? Should I get out and start walking toward the highway? What if someone stopped to help me? Would I be able to trust them? I thought of recent news stories; would I be kidnapped and possibly killed? My palms were clammy as I scanned the horizon for that elusive gas station.

The worst part was, there was no reason for my predicament. The gas gauge was working properly, even so far as giving me a miles-to-go readout (though I was fortunate enough to go five more miles after it showed I had one mile left!). It wasn't that I was broke; I had both cash and a credit card in my purse. There was no excuse except my procrastination. I had been foolish.

As I prayed, a scripture came into mind...the one about the wise virgins and the foolish ones. In the parable, Jesus was talking about something far more important than missing out on a wedding party or even running out of gas. What if the Kingdom of Heaven should catch me unawares? Running out of gas on a good highway in broad daylight isn't the worst thing that could happen to us. What if we were to miss it all just because we failed to make the most important decision of our lifetime?

I coasted into a service station with many a prayer of thanks, but the lesson will stay with me.

We never know when a common predicament can seem like, or even become, a moment of crisis, or when the door of opportunity will be closed for us. May God help us not to procrastinate on the really important choices: to follow the Lord and to keep our lamps trimmed in expectation of the Lord's coming. And one more thing: I don't plan to run on empty ever again.

God has promised forgiveness to your repentance;
But He has not promised tomorrow to your
procrastination.

ST. AUGUSTINE

Thank you, Father, for sending your angels to watch over me even when I make foolish mistakes. Help me to keep fuel in the lamp you have given me and to be ready whenever you call me, even if it is today. Amen.

The Cardinals' Nest

●●●●●●●●●●●●●●●●●●●●●●●●●●●●●●●●●●●●

"The LORD does not look at the things man looks at.
Man looks at the outward appearance, but the LORD
looks at the heart."

1 SAMUEL 16:7B, NIV

For three years, a pair of cardinals nested in a tree near
our living room window. The birds were beautiful, and I
loved watching them. Many cardinals are in our area, as
they do not migrate in the fall, so there would seem to be
nothing unusual about this. Well, that is not quite true.
There was something very unusual. Even though our
yard is lined with trees of many varieties, the tree that
the cardinals chose was of the plastic variety. Yes, that's
right. They built a nest in an artificial (or, as my children
say, fake) tree in one corner of our covered patio. This
seemed strange to me, and I still don't understand it.
While the trees in the yard burst forth each spring with
tender green leaves, the tree on the patio has the same
old dusty leaves perennially. The trees in the backyard
get rinsed with rain every now and then; the plastic tree
does not. The trees in the backyard sway with the breeze;
they drink in the warmth of the sun and draw
nourishment from the ground. So why did the cardinals
choose the plastic tree? My curiosity was great, but I
didn't worry. I simply enjoyed the rare opportunity to
observe them with only a pane of glass separating us. As
I watched, the pair flew busily in and out of the patio,
carrying twigs and other bits of material to build a nest.

●●●●●●●●●●●●●●●●●●●●●●●●●●●●●●●●●●●●

Then I noticed the drabber-colored female sitting on the nest. Ah, I thought, there will soon be baby birds for us to observe. I watched every day, always careful not to intrude or frighten them. Sure enough, one day I noticed a scrawny little neck and head poking above the twigs of the nest. For a time, the birds flew in and out bringing food. Then, suddenly, the baby bird was dead, and before long the pair was gone.

Evidently not quick learners, the cardinals returned to the same nest the next year. Again, a baby bird appeared briefly and then died. And a third time. Never once did a young bird perch expectantly on the edge of the little nest. Never once did one flap its tender wings only to fall awkwardly to the ground. Never once did the cardinals see their offspring fly away from the plastic tree into the big sky that is home to them.

I have often thought about the cardinals. I know little about birds and their habits. I know that the brilliantly colored male was beautiful and that I felt a sense of awe just being so close to this miracle of nature. But somehow, the plastic tree did not provide the right environment for growth and development. Oh, it looked perfect. The leaves were all uniform in shape and size; the sun didn't beat down on the tree; it was further removed from troublesome neighborhood cats; and no other birds were vying for the cardinals' chosen spot. But something was missing. I think it must have been a spiritual thing, an "essence of life" that God puts into all creation.

I miss the birds, and I hope they have found better quarters. In a way, perhaps they learned that the best choices are not always the easy or attractive ones and that outward appearances don't count for much. Fly well, little birds, wherever you are!

> *"For the LORD sees not as man sees; man looks on the outward appearance, but the LORD looks on the heart."*
>
> 1 SAMUEL 16:7B

Thank you, Lord, for the angel hugs you give me through the beauty of nature, and for the lessons they teach. Help me make good decisions, based not on what is easy but on what is good. In the name of the One who cares for the sparrows and for me. Amen.

God Will Keep You

• •

*The LORD delivers him in the day of trouble; the
LORD protects him and keeps him alive.*

PSALMS 41:1B–2

A traditional child's bedtime prayer begins, "Now I lay me down to sleep. I pray thee, Lord, my soul to keep." The childish voices that speak these words may not comprehend their meaning, but sometimes a line will come back to them when they are grown, and the words will take on new meaning.

We all have times when we feel like a cork tossing on turbulent seas, when life turns to chaos and we wonder if we can "keep body and soul together." Difficulties, trouble, and confusion seem to be part of the human condition. Yet, how we handle these difficulties varies greatly from one person to another. We've seen people grow up in tough circumstances, perhaps victims of abuse and neglect, who somehow thrive and turn out to be strong, productive, self-reliant individuals. Others who grow up in these same circumstances never transcend their situations; they merely reflect them and, tragically, repeat them with their own children. Some people can stand firm in the midst of chaos; others "lose it" and blame fate or even God. What a pity to blame God, who instead can help us in such moments!

There's no formula to make trouble evaporate. However, there is help. There is One who will sustain

• •

you, hold your hand and guide you safely through, who will, in fact, *keep your soul*. That someone is the very God who made the universe, who continues to watch over every little sparrow, and who just as surely watches over you.

The apostle Paul led a very exciting life! In a time when many people traveled only a few miles from the place of their birth, he traversed the Mediterranean Sea from Judea to Rome; he traveled around Asia Minor and through many of the islands. As a Christian, his name became so well known that the authorities of the Roman Empire tried to get rid of him. Paul's life was no picnic; he was shipwrecked three times; he was stoned; he was thrown into prison; he was tossed about on the open sea; he suffered from bandits; he suffered from hunger; he was beaten. Compared to his life, the life of an ordinary sea pirate would seem dull! Of course, one difference is that while pirates loot and steal, Paul traveled about with great treasures to give away freely, as he preached the gospel of Christ.

In the face of trouble and danger, Paul stayed the course because he knew that nothing could separate him from God's love. He knew that in all of these things, Christ would keep that which Paul had entrusted to Him.

Surely God, who is changeless from century to century, will sustain you too. He promises this when you accept Him and trust Him. Then you can lie down at night with the simple trust of a child and pray, no matter how turbulent life may seem at the moment, "I pray thee, Lord, my soul to keep."

Living the Beatitudes

• •

> *Seeing the crowds, he went up on the mountain, and*
> *when he sat down his disciples came to him. And he*
> *opened his mouth and taught them, saying: "Blessed*
> *are the poor in spirit, for theirs is the kingdom of*
> *heaven. Blessed are those who mourn, for they shall*
> *be comforted. Blessed are the meek, for they shall*
> *inherit the earth."*
>
> MATTHEW 5:1–5

During the reign of Marilyn Van Derbur as Miss America,
I happened to be in a Minneapolis department store when
she made an appearance. I was eager to meet her because,
apart from the usual reasons, I had represented Oklahoma
in the Miss America pageant the year before. I waited
until her talk was over and was able to visit with her for
a few minutes.

In response to my question about how her year was
going, she told me a delightful story. It seems that she
was to make an appearance in a particular city, and her
chaperone booked a room for her in a fine hotel. Now, I
should tell you that Marilyn Van Derbur, even though
she had won a highly coveted title, was a down-to-earth,
friendly person whose beauty was more like that of the
girl next door. When Marilyn arrived at the hotel, the
maid was in her room.

"Honey, I've got to make this room extra nice, because
Miss America is going to stay here!" the maid exclaimed,
and went bustling about her duties unaware that that

• •

very person stood beside her! I don't know how Marilyn introduced herself, but I am confident that her friendly, gracious manner was a memorable angel hug for the maid.

Do we sometimes look over the shoulder of the person we're with when someone a little more interesting comes into the room? Do we fail to recognize the value of true friendship just because it is familiar? Do we give more credit to glamour than to meekness? Marilyn Van Derbur made a lasting impression on me because she was so real. To me, she will always embody beauty, grace and, yes, meekness in a world where meekness is like a rare jewel.

> *True humility doesn't consist of thinking ill of yourself but of not thinking of yourself much differently from the way you'd be apt to think of anybody else.*
>
> FREDERICK BUECHNER

Thank you, Lord, for those people who really live the teachings of the gospel. Thank you for their example, encouraging me to become the person you would have me be. Amen.

The Grudge: A Fable

• •

> *"So if you are offering your gift at the altar, and*
> *there remember that your brother has something*
> *against you, leave your gift there before the altar and*
> *go; first be reconciled to your brother, and then come*
> *and offer your gift."*
>
> MATTHEW 5:23–24

A man and his friend, meeting at the usual place, had a disagreement. They called each other names, turned away from one another, and parted in anger.

The man was sad, and hurting in his heart. He decided to go for a walk, and happened to pass by the place where the disagreement had occurred. There in the shadows lay a little grudge, the remains of the argument. The thing was poor and weak, and in fact the man hardly noticed it, so insignificant did it appear. Without attention, it surely would have died. The man picked up the grudge and, holding it close to his heart, carried it to the place where he lived.

The man gave the grudge a home, fed it every day, and particularly liked to remember the place of its beginning. The little grudge grew stronger; it became fat and sleek, and soon began to fill up the place where the man lived. Before long, it crowded out some of the more tender occupants like hope, humor, and forgiveness.

Frequently, the man saw his old friend. Sometimes he felt a stirring to invite him into his house for a game of checkers as in the old days, but the grudge filled up

• •

the place so completely that there was no room for such things. The man missed his old friend, but since there was no room he didn't invite him. Anyway, he stayed pretty busy—what with feeding the grudge and remembering the place of its beginning. The only problem was that the grudge had no arms for shaking hands or playing checkers. Still, it was big and strong, and gave the man a certain security. It filled up the hollow spaces and made the man feel bigger.

As time went by, the man continued to feed the grudge, but he gradually began to forget about the place of its beginning, and finally he could not remember it even when he tried. The grudge was very heavy by now, and the man grew tired of carrying it around. In fact, he was so tired that his heart began to hurt again. Perhaps if he had thrown out the grudge, he could have lightened his load and reclaimed the place where hope, humor, and forgiveness used to live. However, this never occurred to him, so he just grew older and more tired, carrying that grudge everywhere he went. The story of the grudge is really amazing; it is remarkable that anything could grow from such an insignificant beginning to such great size and strength, which is all to the credit of the man's tender care and feeding.

To get rid of an enemy, one must love him.

LEO TOLSTOY

Heavenly Father, please forgive me for any grudge I have carried in my heart. Where I have allowed feelings of resentment, help me to send out angel hugs, that I may become the loving person you want me to be. Amen.

Have courage for the great sorrows of life and patience for the small ones; and when you have laboriously accomplished your daily task, go to sleep in peace. God is awake.

VICTOR HUGO

Heavenly Father, I bring you the chaos and turbulence of my life because I cannot manage them, but I know that you can. Help me to trust you completely, to rest in the wonderful knowledge that your love is the angel hug that upholds me no matter what comes my way. Together, Lord, we can make it through anything! In Jesus' name. Amen.

Afterword

There are many people to whom I am grateful for helping make *Angel Hugs* a reality. My deepest appreciation goes to Dr. Robert Schuller for providing the foreword. His positive words have always been a blessing to me, and have helped in my own spiritual growth.

Thanks, also, to Oklahoma's First Lady Cathy Keating, to Dr. Jerald Walker, Jane Jayroe, and Dr. Norman Neaves for their generous endorsements for the book jacket.

I am deeply indebted to my dear friend, the late Dr. J. Clyde Wheeler, who urged me to write this book. His words of encouragement will always be remembered.

Thanks to Charles Bruner and Val Thiessen for their help with the manuscript, to Mo Grotjohn, and to Judge Robert Henry, who found the devotionals encouraging and inspiring. Another big thanks goes to Patti Case, who helped make *Angel Hugs* a reality.

Thanks to my family for believing in me, and especially for letting me write about them. Finally, love and thanks to my husband Herman for his steadfast support and encouragement. Angel hugs to all of you!

LaDonna Meinders